Color Patterns Of Zen

Fun Coloring Book For Adults
Book I

Yael Ben-Ari

Color Patterns Of Zen
Fun Coloring Book For Adults Book I

Yael Ben-Ari

Illustrations, design, and writing © Yael Ben-Ari 2016
www.DontWannaGrowup.com

All Rights Reserved. No part of this book may be reproduced or transmitted in any form or by any means, including, but not limited to information storage and retrieval systems, electronic, mechanical, photocopy, recording, etc., without express written permission from the author and copyright holder.

Dedication

This Book is dedicated to my family,
friends, and all Big Kids who
Don't Wanna Grow Up.

How To Use This Book

This book is for big kids who Don't Wanna Grow Up. It's for having a fun and a relaxing time coloring. Be creative. Color outside the lines or inside the lines as you see fit. Make new lines where there are none or combine coloring areas. It's up to you.

The images are all hand drawn with a little help from the artist's computer, so there may be irregular lines and spaces. Add your own personal touches and originality to make truly one-of-a-kind creations.

If you are using markers, or other wet media, be sure to use a piece of heavy paper underneath the page you are working on to avoid bleeding through to the next page.

By all means, take the book apart, so you can color more easily and display what you have done.

Above all, Have Fun!

* Be sure to visit our website, DontWannaGrowUp.com for tips on coloring and what's new from the Author.
* Follow Us on Twitter: twitter.com/DontWannaGrowP)
* Books by this author on Amazon: Author.to/YaelBenAri

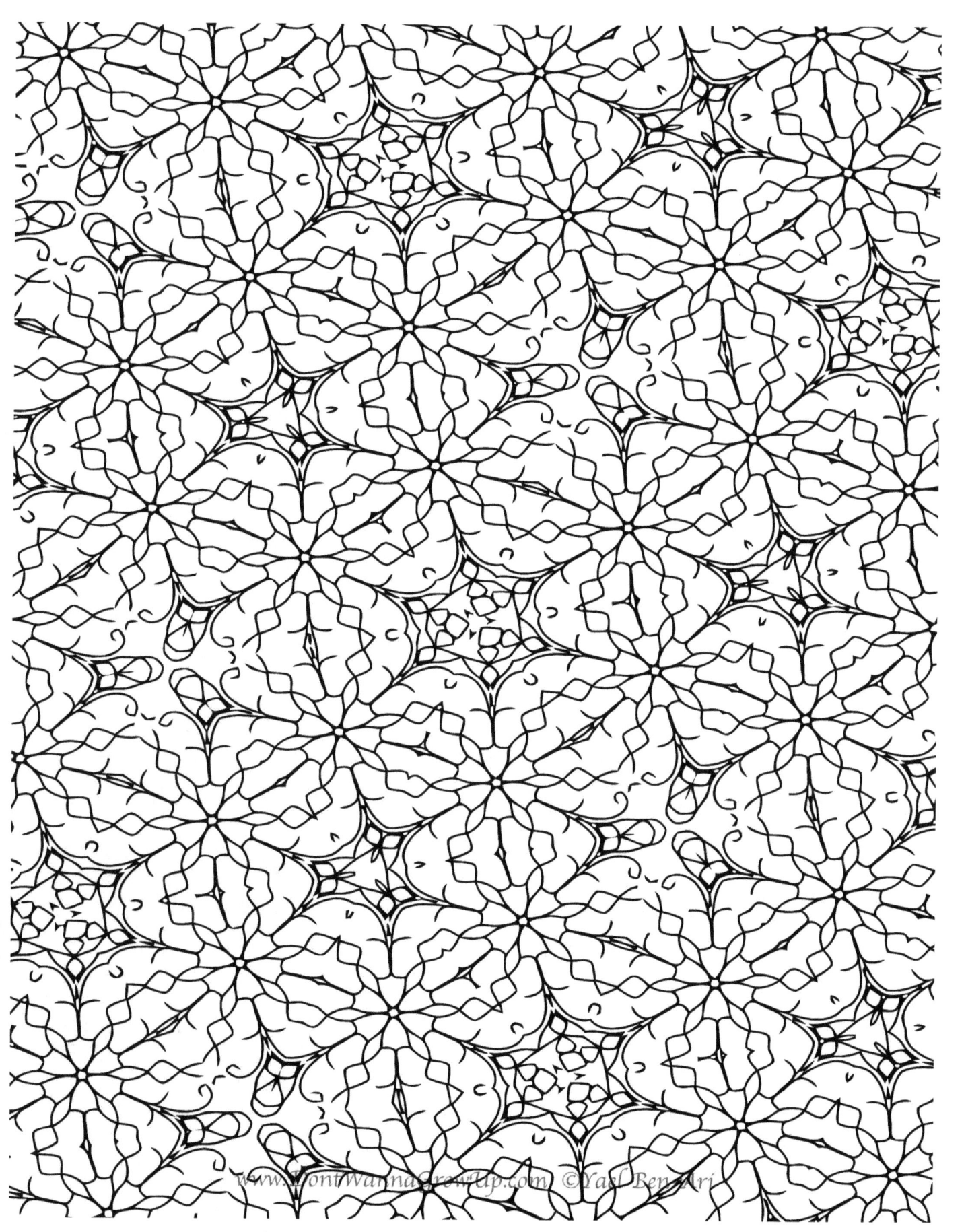

Books By Yael Ben-Ari
Collect Them All

 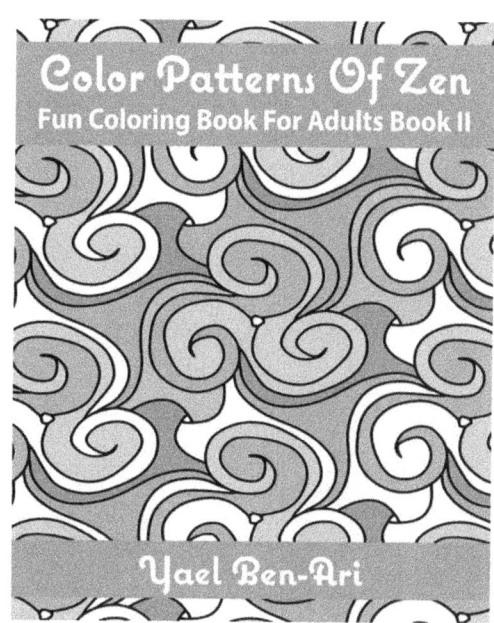

Find books by this Author on Amazon: Author.to/YaelBenAri

And come on over to www.DontWannaGrowUp.com
for some Free Coloring Pages, too.

I hope you enjoy them and leave a review after the book comes.

www.ingramcontent.com/pod-product-compliance
Lightning Source LLC
Chambersburg PA
CBHW081018040426
42444CB00014B/3258